Begin your Moonlight journey today with a FREE copy of **MOONLIGHT FALLS**, the first novel in the Thriller and Shamus Award winning series. Or visit **WWW.VINZANDRI.COM** to join Vincent's "For your eyes only" newsletter today.

PRAISE FOR VINCENT ZANDRI

"Sensational . . . masterful . . . brilliant."
—New York Post

"(A) chilling tale of obsessive love from Thriller Award–winner Zandri (Moonlight Weeps) . . . Riveting."
—Publishers Weekly

". . . Oh, what a story it is . . . Riveting . . . A terrific old school thriller."
—Booklist "Starred Review"

"Zandri does a fantastic job with this story. Not only does he scare the reader, but the horror Show he presents also scares the man who is the definition of the word "tough."
—Suspense Magazine

"I very highly recommend this book . . . It's a great crime drama that is full of action and intense suspense, along with some great twists . . . Vincent Zandri has become a huge name and just keeps pouring out one best seller after another."
—Life in Review

'(The Innocent) is a thriller that has depth and substance, wickedness and compassion."
—The Times-Union (Albany)

'The action never wanes."
—Fort Lauderdale Sun-Sentinel

"Gritty, fast-paced, lyrical and haunting."
—Harlan Coben, New York Times bestselling author of *Six Years*

"Tough, stylish, heartbreaking."
—Don Winslow, New York Times bestselling author of *Savages* and *Cartel*.

"A tightly crafted, smart, disturbing, elegantly crafted complex thriller . . . I dare you to start it and not keep reading."
—MJ Rose, New York Times bestselling author of *Halo Effect* and *Closure*

"A classic slice of raw pulp noir…"
—William Landay, New York Times bestselling author of *Defending Jacob*

The Hybrid Author Mindset:

The totally honest, no BS, myth-busting, realistic, non-politically correct guide to succeeding at publishing traditionally and independently and making a very good passive income.

Vincent Zandri

"The story of Vincent Zandri is the story of our times."
--Business Insider

"Vincent Zandri is one of the most acclaimed thriller writers working today!"

-- Publishers Weekly

Part I

A very personal publishing story

I'm one of the lucky ones. Or unlucky ones, depending on how you look at it now. Just six months out of writing school I nail a $250K contract with a major publisher in a two book deal, beginning with the hard-boiled novel I wrote while in writing school, The Innocent. It's not a dream come true, it's *the* dream come true. For me, it's immediate success and validation right out of the starting gate. I'm barely 33 years old, and I'm up to my neck in student loan and credit card debt. I've got a stay-at-home wife and two toddlers running around, and the money I'm making as a freelance journalist and writer is barely keeping a roof over our heads much less beer in the ice box.

But now, with this new deal, I can not only pay everything off, I can quit freelancing altogether and concentrate on the fiction exclusively. Unbeknownst to me at the time, it will be one of the worst decisions of my life.

But more on that later.

I'm on top of the world. Reporters are coming out of the woodwork to interview me. Publishers Weekly features me in not one story, but two. People are sending me congratulatory Hallmark cards, and even some of my writing professors pat me on the back (however reluctantly. In full disclosure, one of them says it's too early for me. How right he was.) Movie producers are calling and so are actors like George Clooney and Robert DeNiro. I'm over the moon.

My agent, Sweet Talking Jimmy V and I hit the town (Manhattan that is) like rock stars. We binge drink and party well into the night. He takes me for fancy dinners at famous steakhouses. We smoke cigars and flirt with the women. Sometimes the flirting leads to something else. I hand bellhops one-hundred dollar bills to see to my every need, including a fully stocked bar. There's cocaine, brain buds, champagne, parties up in my suite at the Gramercy Park Hotel with other agents, publishers, and writers. I start a rock band with my editor and I enter into a brief, consensual affair with my publicist. It's like a bacchanalian scene out of an old Norman Mailer movie.

My editor, Jake, does his magic with The Innocent, and I respond with a terrific rewrite. Everything is set for publication. All barrels locked and loaded. Except for one small detail. He wants to change the title since it's already in use by another Delacorte author. The title he goes with is…wait for it…As Catch Can. It comes from an old Blue Note jazz standard. I mull it around in my brain. I hate it. But I love my editor. I'm too much of a newbie to realize it's okay to disagree with your editor. So I go with the title change. It will be another decision that will come to haunt me in the very near future.

In those days it took a long time for a book to get published. I first got word of the As Catch Can acceptance by Delacorte in late October of 1997 (it had gone to auction, the bidders having been Random House and St. Martins Press. In retrospect I should have taken the slightly lesser offer initiated by Charlie Spicer at St. Martins, who is still in the business and still loyal to his authors). But the pub date was set for February of 1999. For a young man, that is a lifetime away. But that's the snail's pace the traditional writing game runs at and still runs at. It's entirely the opposite of indie publishing whereby you write your book, send it off to editing and formatting, produce a high quality cover for eBook, audio, and trade paper, and immediately get the book into production. It's not unheard of in indie world to write a 60K word novel one month, have it edited and produced the next month, and by the end of that second month, have it released to the world. Some writers are able to produce 12 or more novels with this method and at the same time, retaining the copyrights forever and ever.

But in traditional world, you wait and wait and wait, and wait some more. But hey, if they're giving you a quarter of a million dollars, you enjoy the wait. And boy oh boy, did I enjoy the wait. First thing I did was quit my job at my dad's construction business for good, while at the same time, ditching my freelance writing clients. I also took a break from writing fiction for a while. I figured I would be enjoying huge advances for the rest of my days from that point on, so why worry and most of all, why write if I didn't have to? In fact, I recall to this day my editor telling me to take a break. Can you imagine in this, the new golden age of pulp fiction, taking a break from your writing? If anything, I find myself not being able to keep up with my own projects. There's never enough time in the day to take care of everything.

But like a knucklehead I cut off all the ties I had to my lucrative freelance accounts and freed myself up to pretty much spend my days working out during the daylight hours and partying in the evening. It was a life of luxury come way too soon and totally undeserved. In a word, I was setting the stage for my own demise.

Then comes the big day. Publication day. As Catch Can is released to the world. It immediately garners stellar reviews from the likes of Publisher Weekly, Booklist, Kirkus Reviews, The Boston Herald, and more. It earns killer blurbs by Don Winslow and Harlan Coben. The New York Post calls As Catch Can, "Sensational . . . masterful . . . brilliant." I do the TV circuit and dozens of book signings. I share a cab with Harlan Coben in Philly, and drink beers with Otto Penzler inside his back office in lower Manhattan's Mysterious Bookshop. I also spend $12K on one of the best outside publicists in the business.

What can go wrong?

I'm so confident that As Catch Can is going to knock it out of the park and earn me a number one spot on the New York Times bestseller list, I sell my humble bungalow, and move the family into a new big house in Albany's wealthy hamlet of Loudonville. It costs me most of my initial advance, but so what. I'm about to become a millionaire. My wife joins an expensive gym and hires a personal trainer. I buy a new truck and we splurge expensive vacations, all with the expectation that "Catch" is going to catch on like wild fire.

But something else happens instead. The big yawn. Despite outstanding reviews and distribution, nobody is buying the book. What gives? It could be the title (whenever I tell somebody the title of my new novel, they inevitably look at me cross-eyed and say, "What?" They then remember the title not as, As Catch Can, but instead, Catch as Catch Can. It's a real problem.)

Could it be the cover?

Later on, one Delacorte Press exec will admit to me that the cover was botched (it was redone entirely for the mass market paperback).

But in the end, it's more than likely another problem plagues my novel. Delacorte is going through an internal upheaval. A major consolidation is happening. That means lots of editors, publicists, and authors are about to be shown the door. When I arrive in New York one sunny day to meet up with my editor in his Bertelsmann Building office in Times Square, I run into my editor in chief in the lobby. She's holding her desk lamp in her hand, and she's crying. She hugs me, kisses me on the cheek, and whispers, "Good luck." But what she really means is, "Rest in peace." Within a few months, I find out my contract with Delacorte will not be renewed. I will be back to square one.

I've got a new house, a new mortgage, no new money coming in, and I haven't even paid my taxes yet. It's like the earth has opened up under my feet and swallowed me whole.

The same writing prof who said it was too soon for me to enjoy that kind of success also told me this. "This is a business of two steps forward, three steps back." I wasn't sure what he meant until I was let go from Delacorte with my tail between my legs. It's not three steps back, but one-hundred. One-thousand. I leave most of the $250K advance unredeemed, which means no other major publisher will take me on even at gunpoint. Delacorte honors their contract by paying me all my monies and bringing out my second novel, but like many people who win the lottery, I soon find myself going broke, and fast.

My original advance is mostly spent and there's no money coming in since I ditched all my freelance clients and any hope of rejoining the family business is long faded. I can't afford the mortgage on the new house. Can't afford the quarterly taxes and the credit cards bills. I begin to hit the bottle. I lose weight. Something else is happening too. Something nefarious. My wife asks me for a divorce, and what follows is a nasty breakup that not only costs me everything I have left, but if it isn't for the generous financial assistance of my late father, I'd go bankrupt. I placed all my eggs in one basket, and the basket burned up in a fiery blaze. I'm a hot mess, and what just a year earlier seemed like a dream come true, turns out to be my worst nightmare.

Fast forward a few years. I'm single again after a brief marriage to a woman who I thought of as the love of my life. I'm living in a 1,000 square foot apartment with my two sons. I'm back to being a freelance journalist, writing for global publications like *RT*, and traveling the world to exotic places including West Africa, China, Russia, South America, India, and of course Europe. I begin spending the fall season in Florence, Italy. Something I still do to this day. I'm making a living, however humble. I guess you can I'm working my way back up the ladder.

I'm also back to writing crime novels. My new agent suggests we attempt to get the rights back to my first two novels at Delacorte and republish them with a new publisher. The new publisher is heavily into eBooks, something that has just come onto the scene in conjunction with Amazon's release of the Kindle eReader. I have no idea what the hell a Kindle is. But my agent tells me that if we can get the rights back to As Catch Can and its follow up, Godchild, we'll get it republished in just a matter of months.

A matter of months. How can that be? I'm told that in the digital world, there isn't the wait that there is for paper. A novel can be uploaded literally in a matter of minutes and delivered directly to the readers. No longer is it necessary to wait many months or even years for the paper version to get processed. Clearly, this is brand new revolutionary territory we're dealing with here and it's blowing my mind.

To my amazement, Delacorte agrees to give me back my rights. While I continue to bang out my journalism stories and freelance copy, As Catch Can, is republished by this new upstart independent publisher. We've changed the title back to The Innocent, and the new cover is spectacular if not stunning. It's everything the novel should have been during its initial publication back in 1999.

Truth be told however, I don't have high hopes for the book. I mean, it's twelve years old already. Who the hell is going to invest their hard-earned coin on an old novel?

But something wonderful happens. The Innocent not only begins to sell, it goes ballistic, selling 100K units in just five weeks. Godchild, edition two, is rushed into publication, and it too sells in the tens of thousands of units. Then comes a brand new novel, The Remains. It will sell in the tens of thousands and go on to sell 200K units and counting. Suddenly, I'm back on top of the fiction world. Suddenly, I'm making far more money with my fiction than my freelance writing. The big irony is that I will make enough in just a few short months to earn out my original $250K Delacorte advance.

For the first time in a dozen years, I have more money in the bank than I do debt.

The major publishers start calling again. I'm offered a considerable advance for five new books from one of Amazon Publishing's imprints, Thomas & Mercer. Since they're the new powerhouse crime publisher on the block, I gladly accept. I also accept deals from smaller crime imprints like Polis Books and Down & Out Books. Suddenly, I'm being written about by the New York Times, Business Insider, and Publishers Weekly (again). Suddenly I'm appearing on Bloomberg TV and the Fox News Network (yeah, that's right, *the* Fox news). Suddenly, I'm someone again.

It took more than a decade, but I'd come full circle.

At this point, I might have repeated my initial blunder and chucked the journalism altogether, while concentrating only on the fiction. But I learned from the past that to keep all of one's eggs in one basket (there's that horse flogged metaphor again) is death to any writer. I sit down and attempt to figure out the best way to balance my time between freelance writing and fiction writing. As I'm doing this, something else begins to dawn on me. If the publishers, both big and small who rely largely on Amazon to move units, can achieve success, why can't I achieve it on my own? Or heck, why can't I do both? What I don't realize at the time, is that I'm about to become a hybrid author, whether I know it or not.

In a nutshell, the hybrid author works with both the traditional publishing model and the new independent publishing model wherein, one self-publishes a series of titles under one's own publishing label. In my case, Bear Media, LLC. By becoming a hybrid, I not only enjoy the benefits of traditional publishing, like terrific distribution, trade and major media reviews, plus a presence in bookstores and libraries, I'm also building a sort of real estate empire of my own titles. Most importantly, I'm creating multiple sources of income, if not passive income, that will generate both cash flow and something that was once impossible for any professional crime writer prior to the digital publishing revolution of 2008: Security!

Books as real estate. Sounds strange doesn't it? But unlike the traditional publishing model, in which a book enjoys a short shelf life in a brick and mortar bookstore until it is pulled and replaced by something new, the independently produced book is reliant heavily on eBook sales.

Perhaps you invest $2,000 in the production of one single 60-90K word title. Say that title earns you only $100 per month. That's $1,200 per year. Not enough to live on, but what if you had ten independent books earning you $100 per month? That's $12,000 annually with an initial investment of $20,000. After only two years, you've not only paid off your initial investment, you are now solidly in the black. Try making that kind of return by stocking $20K away in a CD or mutual fund account.

As I come to realize the enormous financial opportunities hybrid authorship offers me, I also begin to realize something else. I'm no longer a slave to the old system of query and hope. I will never again be subject to the whims and/or failing business model of one single publisher. If a publisher only wants one book per year, well hell, Bear Media can publish ten, or even twenty. If the publisher is undergoing a consolidation and I'm released because of it, no problem, I have other lucrative sources of income. If a publisher chooses not to take on a new novel for one reason or another, I can always publish it under my own label. This has happened to me a couple of times now, and both titles sell very well as Bear Media productions (in fact, one of them, Scream Catcher, I resold to Polis Books, much to my regret). In other words, the mantra for the modern day hybrid crime author has changed. It's no longer, *if* my novel gets published. It's *how* my novel will get published. And trust me, the reader doesn't give a crap if the novel spine says Delacorte Press or Bear Media. The readers only cares if it's a great book.

The possibilities of hybrid authorship are enormous. Not only does it offer a publishing safety net for your work, it also offers a creative safety net. In this new world, a writer no longer must be bound by length, style, genre, or point of view. In other words, you can write whatever the hell you want, how you want, when you want. If you have an idea for a novel that a publisher would never touch, then go for it. For instance, if you want to finally write that western vampire erotica novel, go for it. A traditional publisher would never touch it, but you can produce it under your own label. And believe me, there will be an audience for it. Maybe not a huge one, but the indie side of things isn't about making enormous sales right away. It's about slow growth and the accumulation of small numbers over time. You've seen the drain spout that fills the water barrel, one drip at a time. That's the indie part of hybrid authorship.

Which leads me to…

…One big ass caveat. Hybrid authorship is not a get rich quick scheme. It is a business model that favors long-term growth. Sure, there will always be some lucky, right out of writing school kid who manages to nail a mid-six figure contract and who becomes an overnight rock star sensation (sound familiar?), but these moments are fleeting and often result in disastrous consequences. A hybrid author should not expect to turn over a significant profit for maybe five years of continuous production. Unless you already have a significant savings stocked away, you will be using your advances from your traditional deals to help pay for the production of your indie books. This means paying a team of cover artists and editors. Why put up the cash to pay these professionals? Because the independently produced books must be at least as good as the traditionally produced book, if not better.

The hybrid author must also be prolific. If you can't write at least 2k new words per day on average of new material, day in and day out, five to six days per week, you are doomed. You must shift your mindset to one of artist to businessperson. The writing is the art, but the production and marketing of your independent books is strictly business. Get used to it, or if running a business doesn't appeal to you, then stick to traditional publishing exclusively and make sure you have a day job just in case things don't work out.

Just the other day, one of my publishers emailed me with concern over my independent publishing schedule. He feared I was undercutting sales of the books that he owned the rights to.

Fair enough, but I reminded him that unless I continue to put out titles under my own label, I risk losing money and significant return on investment. In the end I agreed to inform him of upcoming pub dates which consists of at least one novel or novella per month for the remainder of the year. He then went on to quiz me about marketing and promotions. What works and what doesn't work. How can he sell more titles? What's his firm doing wrong? It was a strange turn of events, the publisher coming to the writer for advice.

Was a time the writer had no power. We were relegated to the bottom of the totem pole. Agents, publishers, even bookstores could accept or reject us depending upon their mood or the weather. But today, with the digital revolution, all that has changed and it's flipped the traditional model onto its back. This is a golden age of writing not realized since the pulp fiction days of the 1930s, 40s, and 50s, when an author could write for a penny per word and make millions.

It amazes me the writers who still cling to the all-or-nothing dream of acceptance by the big publisher. Talented writers who instead of worrying and biting their cuticles off, could be using that time and energy to focus on writing more stories, publishing them, earning on them, and more importantly, building an audience. Why do they place their hopes and dreams in one basket? Why don't they become hybrid and guarantee themselves a passive income not only for themselves, but for their children, and their children's children? It boggles the mind.

But one things is for sure, hybrid authorship is damned hard work. You will have to work your tail off to produce many titles while keeping your traditional publishers and their ever constricting contracts happy. But in the end you will enjoy the security of knowing there is money coming in and significant return on investment. All you have to do is write, publish, rinse, repeat. Sounds easy, but it's damned hard, at least in the short-term. Now stop reading this and get to work.

Part II

Traditional publishing vs. indie publishing: Myths Debunked or should I say, The Truth Revealed.

Validation

Traditional:

Most writers crave validation for their efforts. No, that's not right. They lust validation. We want not only to sell, but to feel validation from our peers. We want to be respected as 'real writers.' That's exactly what happens when a traditional publisher makes an offer for your novel. Your talent is being validated. If you win a prestigious award and nail one of the bestseller lists like The New York Times or USA Today on behalf of your efforts, then you've reached the apex of validation.

People look at you differently after you've signed a major book deal. You carry yourself differently. You are more confident. You look and feel more attractive to the world. You've gripped the world by the shorthairs and everyone knows it. But a word of caution here. The confidence can be terribly short-lived if, upon publication, the book tanks. I've been there. Take my word for it.

Indie:

No one is going to root for you when you self-publish a stand-alone title or a series. It might collect loyal fans, and it might garner great customer reviews, and it might even be written about in a blog or two, but more than likely, you are not going to hit any of the bestseller lists (aside from Amazon), nor are you going to win any awards. There are exceptions to this, of course. Some indie books go on to be mega sellers and gain the attention of Hollywood. Andy Weir's, The Martian, and EL James's, 50 Shades of Grey, come immediately to mind.

Indie publishing is just that. You are creating and producing your work independent of the status quo, or in today's jargon, the swamp. The nature of the beast is that you are going it alone, without acclaim, critical or otherwise. Get used to people asking you if you're still writing. It's not that they're living under a rock, it's just that they don't and won't see your books prominently displayed in the Barnes and Nobles.

However, what they don't know, is that your indie books are making you a nice little handsome return on investment. You could try telling them that, but they're just going to look at you cross-eyed.

Freedom

Traditional:

In traditional world you are going to sign a contract that will pretty much give away all your publishing rights. Sure, there are some instances whereby those mega-Kindle eBook sellers can find a way to maintain their eBook rights while signing a "paper only" deal with a major house, but those instances are so few and far between as to be non-existent. The entire idea behind signing with a major house is that they take charge over the creative process of your work while owning your work forever. One does this in exchange for an advance which, hopefully, will be sizeable enough for you to enjoy the "freedom" to write for a while. You also get exceptional editing and copyediting, a really cool cover (one hopes), and some expert marketing from the publisher's marketing department.

In theory, that is.

These days, much of the marketing is left up to the authors. In summary, when one signs with a traditional publisher you lose most of your freedom including the publishing rights to your book. You do this in exchange for a check, which should allow you the freedom to write full-time for maybe a year or so. If your book doesn't sell enough to earn out the advance, you will never receive another penny from that book again. Nor is it likely that you will sign another contract with that publisher. Have a nice life.

Indie:

You don't sign squat. You own all your publishing rights. You write whatever you want, when you want, how you want, for as long as you want. If you are putting out a series, the series never gets cancelled because of slow sales (for the most part, you can count on indie sales to be SLOW but steady). You retain all the rights to your stories forever and ever. When you die, your children will hold the rights, and eventually, their children, all of whom will receive a nice passive income month after month, so long as the books are maintained and occasionally placed in promos. You have the freedom do things however you see fit. You are commander of your ship, and of yeah, you own the freaking ship too.

In exchange for this freedom however, you are going to be making a significant financial investment. Indie publishing is art but it is also a business too. The investment you make in creating your 60,000 to 80,000 word novel/non-fiction book will likely be anywhere from $1,500 to $2,500 depending upon the quality of your cover artists and editors. And trust me, you don't want to skimp on any of this (I have a terrific editorial team behind me). In fact, my rule for putting out indie books under my label, Bear Media, is this: If the book isn't equal to or better than my traditional books, it doesn't get published. End of story, full stop. Which leads me to …

Investment

Traditional:

You're not making any significant financial investment in the production of your book. The publisher does that instead when they give you a check upon contract signing and later on when you deliver the revised manuscript (A little cold sober warning here. I've seen book contracts canceled when the author couldn't rewrite the novel according to the acquiring editor's critique which usually arrives in the form of a long editorial letter and accompanying bullet points. If this happens, it can spell disaster for a career. The NYC publishing community is small. Editors and agents talk). You will however, be making the investment of time and some money when it comes to marketing. Investment is not quite the right word here, because by putting up money to say, hire an expensive publicist for example, you're not making an investment in yourself so much as the publisher's bottom line.

I hired one of the best publicists in New York for my first big novel, As Catch Can. It cost me well over $12K and the firm *didn't do shit*, as the expression goes. I'll never get that 12 grand back, but lesson learned. In very rare cases, a novel will become a blowout sensation, which will lead to more lucrative publishing contracts along with foreign rights and movie contracts. In this very rare case, the time investment you put in by writing your novel was worth every penny and then some.

You will, in a word, have made the big time.

Indie:

I hate to break it to you, but if indie publishing is one thing above anything else, it is most definitely not glamorous. There's no exciting call from the agent telling you your novel is about to go up for auction with all the NYC houses. There's no mega advance, or Amtrak-train-ride-down-to-the-Big-Apple for celebratory drinks. There's no big skyscrapers in Times Square, no pre-pub announcement in Publishers Weekly. No newspaper articles, no calls from the friends, no teary congrats calls from your mom (In rare circumstances your indie book will sell so well that a major publisher will snatch it up in exchange for a very nice advance. This has also happened to me). You're not in it for the glory but for the business investment and personal (very personal) artistic gain. However, despite the absence of glam what you get in return for your financial investment is solid, passive income growth.

Here's some math.

Say your book cost you $2,000 to create and publish. Say you're selling that book for 3.99. Since Kindle Direct Publishing and most other platforms offer a 70% royalty per eBook copy sold, that's a $2.793 per sale, net profit. Now let's be as conservative as possible, and say you sell 20 copies per month. That's $55.86 pure profit. Per year that amounts to $670.32. No traditional publisher would even glance at a book that sold so poorly. But in indie land, that's a very nice annual take home pay. Amazingly it represents a 34% return on investment, or what's commonly known as ROI (if you plan on going indie or hybrid, get used to those three letters).

Taken a step further, if you have 10 products (novels, bundles, short story collections, non-fiction books, etc.) priced at 3.99 that sell conservatively and average twenty full-priced sales per month, that amounts to $6,703.20. Okay, so now we're getting into real money. Not enough to quit your job yet (unless you have another passive income), but nothing to sneeze at. Listen, I've suffered through more than my fair share of years back when I was entirely traditional, when I made nothing on my fiction. Not a dime. And that's after having enjoyed major contracts from major publishers.

Finally, what if you have 20 products priced at $3.99 selling conservatively at 20 copies per month every month on average. That's $13,406.40. Now you're getting close to quitting your job if you live in a cheap part of the country. If you live as an expat in Mexico or Asia you can live like a king or queen on this. By the way, a book that moves only 20 eBook editions per month will rank in the hundreds of thousands. 30 products will get you $20,109.60. And 40 products will bring in $26,812.8. And so on. I know of some indie authors who have 100 book products and counting. It's a numbers game folks and yes, it's all about the content.

But here's the thing. That final number is probably low since the more products you have the more you are going to sell and the more your profits should rise exponentially, not algebraically. Think of indie sales as almost like a pyramid scheme. The more products you have under your belt, the more you're going to make. When you include profits from audio (which is becoming huge) plus KDP and/or Createspace print, and even affiliate sales from Amazon Associates, you begin to see something amazing happening. You are creating a passive income that will far outlast any traditional contract.

It is a case of putting in the work and putting out more and more great content that is professionally edited and outfitted with a fantastic eye-grabbing cover. What's more, you own your own rights and you have the freedom to do whatever you want with your books. If you want to put out a special editors cut extended version (like I did with Moonlight Falls), you can do it. If you wish to relaunch a five year special edition, you have the freedom to do that too. There's no stopping you, other than the limits of your imagination.

But is it glamorous?

No.

You're not even hitting many if any Amazon bestseller lists. But what you are doing is earning a terrific return on your initial investment while retaining all your publishing rights and publishing power. The key, is to always think conservatively, and always think in terms of averages. Simply put, some books are going to sell more than others, while some books won't sell much at all. On the other hand, some books will miraculously sell very well regardless of whether you actively promote them or not. That's called luck (Never underestimate the power of luck. Like they say, the harder you work, the more lucky you get). That is the nature of this beast. Feed the beast with more and more words and books, and the beast will reward you in spades.

Proliferation

Traditional:

Traditional publishers don't want you writing. At base, a traditional house wants one book per year and only one book. There are several reasons for this. A publishing house is essentially a mega goliath of editors, artists, marketing personnel, bean counters, you name it. They work high up inside a steel and glass tower (the Bertelsmann Building), and it costs them thousands just to turn the lights on every morning. Your book is just another expenditure in a sea of expenditures.

Lots of…let's call them publishing professionals…will want a say in how your book gets to see the light of day. Everyone from the accountants to the foreign rights department will need some time with it, which means with all this bureaucratic swamp-like inefficiency running amok, it takes a year or sometimes more for the book to go through several rounds of edits and finally make the trip to the printing press.

Writers, when signing major contracts, need to be weary (and beware) of clauses that prohibit the author from publishing any other books that might compete with the contracted book for shelf space. This essentially hogties a writer and limits their income potential. Writers, like me, who are prolific and can write a novel in a single month, have trouble with this aspect of the traditional model because I can write way more than one book per year. Truth is if I don't write more than one book per year, I'm doomed financially. That's why most writers who publish exclusively with the Big 5 (or is it Big 4 now?), must maintain a day job while lots of hybrid and indie authors write for a living.

Which way would you rather live your life?

Indie:

Like I just said, I can write a 40,000-60,000 novel in about a month. Some novels, especially the longer (80,000 to 100,000 words), more literary psychological suspense standalones might take two months. A short story of up to 5,000 words might take a single day. A novella of anywhere between 10,000 and 20,000 words might take a week but no more than two. A 30,000 word short novel can take three weeks and another week to produce a final rewrite. What all this means, of course, is that I am able to put out a lot of good to great material, fast. There are indie and hybrid writers who are faster than me. Much faster. They write at what bestselling genre author Dean Wesley Smith has coined, Pulp Speed. That is, around 5,000 words per day, six days a week. At that speed, you can write a full 60,000 word novel in a week. And get this, you can do it easily.

I write full-time, but that doesn't mean I sit at the laptop for eight hours per day. Far from it. I write utilizing the sprint method. In other words, I do maybe three to four half-hour to hour long sprints per day in which I produce anywhere from 500 to 1200 words. By the end of the day, I've written anywhere from 2,000 to 3,000+ words. You might be a little slower or a little faster. It's all up to the individual.

But the point is, a professional writer should be writing every day. That's how many of the pulp writers of the 1920s, 30s, 40s, and 50s became rich—by writing tons of words, day in and day out, and getting paid by the word by the pulp magazines. It wasn't until the 1970s that the big establishment publishers began demanding that writers only put out one book per year. That ushered out the pulp era and began a new era whereby writers were no longer in control of their careers. But now, in this new digital age, writers are back in control and can decide for themselves how to publish. That's why I choose to be a hybrid author, because I get the best of both worlds--the notoriety and acclaim that comes from traditional world, and the solid investment and passive income that comes from indie world.

The point to all this, is that I am able to put out way more than one book per year. Each book or product I put out makes me money. Money I need to live and save and travel and eventually to pass on to my children. Speaking of which…

Financials

Traditional:

So you finally nailed the big contract. Your agent just called, all out of breath and beyond excited. She can hardly wait to tell you that you have been offered $100,000 for a two book, hardback, soft, eBook, and audio world rights deal. You're about to become the darling of New York City and the talk of the town. You're do excited, you scream! All your office workers become so alarmed they think someone has died. But the only thing that's died is your need for a day job. Everyone is so excited for you they take you out for drinks at Happy Hour.

So here's what happens over the course of the next few months. You sign the big contract. In turn, your agent sends you the signing portion of the advance. Since this contract is for $100K that means it's $50K per book. The signing portion of the first advance might be $25,000. That sounds like a lot and it is a lot. But after the agent takes her 15% you are down to $21,250. Next in line is Uncle Sam and his cut which, if you have a good accountant and get lucky, might be 25%. Now you're down to $15,937.50. Okay, still not bad. But conservatively speaking, if it costs you $4,000 per month to live, you're going to run out of money in just little bit shy of four months. If you have a savings put away, you'll have to start digging into it. If you don't have a savings, you might have to start thinking about asking your boss for your old job back. But you would rather hang from the ceiling by your fingernails than do that. You're about to be a mega bestseller. Everyone thinks you're a major success, even before the book is released. You have your pride to think about.

Plus you have another $25K coming for the first book, right? So what's to worry about? You pull out the credit cards and cover yourself until you get the next round of monies. Easy Peasy. That next round of cash comes in say, six or eight months down the road when you deliver your revised manuscript. If…the important word is IF here…your revised manuscript is accepted, you will receive the Delivery and Acceptance portion of your first advance.

Let's say the D&A is $12,500. After you do all the math you're left with about $7K and change. That might last you two months if you stretch it out. It most certainly doesn't cover the credit card balances you've been racking up. But you're stubborn and you look forward to the next and final portion of your advance which will arrive on publication day…

…four months later.

Okay, so it's the big day you've been waiting for. Publication day. You just got a nice check for $12,500 minus the agent's fee (You've decided to forgo Uncle Sam's portion on this one, because your book is going to be a bestseller and you'll earn out the initial $50K in a matter of weeks when the book lands on the New York Times bestseller list). You have a check in your pocket for $10,625 and even if your credit card balance is more than that (and don't forget the back taxes), you feel on top of the world.

Your author copies arrive, you take a ton of selfies for Facebook and Instagram, you collect a ton of "likes", you do a couple signings in your hometown, and maybe, just maybe if you live in proximity to NYC, you do a signing at the B&N in Union Square. The reviews come out and in general they are very kind. Maybe you didn't get the New York Times review you were dreaming of, but you did get one in People and another in Entertainment Weekly. In a word, you are a rock star.

Then something happens…The Big Yawn.

Your book doesn't make the New York Times bestseller list. It doesn't even make the USA Today bestseller list which is easier. But it does make several Amazon lists which is encouraging, or so your editor tells you over the phone. The troubling thing however, is that as time goes on, you notice your conversations with both your editor and agent are becoming shorter and shorter. They don't seem to be as emotionally invested as they once were. It's troubling because even before your second book in the contract comes out, you realize you desperately need another very big contract in order to get yourself out of debt.

You go to work on the next novel. You write frantically and finish it in record time. You deliver it to your editor. You don't hear from him for weeks, or even months. You email him and your agent incessantly. Finally, the editor emails you back. He says he's read the book and "likes" it. However, seeing as it looks like you're not going to earn out the first half of your advance, they are going to forgo the hardback publication and go straight to mass market paper and eBook. You feel your heart drop into your stomach. How are you going to break the news to your wife and your mother?

The year goes buy and you receive the balance of your $100,000 contact, or $50,000. After your agent takes what he's owed, you make the horrible decision to keep the entire $42,500 since you're in such debt you can't possibly pay the $10,000+ plus federal and state tax bill owed. As it is, you already owe more than $5K to the IRS from the previous advance check.

You call your editor. He takes the call which is encouraging. You tell him about your next book project…a high concept thriller. But all you get is dead air, which is not only discouraging, it is downright disconcerting. He calmly explains to you that it's probably in your best interest to pursue another publisher for your next book project. He hangs up. You'll never hear from him again.

After living on the $42,500 for the year, you are dead broke, in serious debt to the credit card companies, and the IRS. Your agent and editor don't return your phone calls or emails. You don't have a job or any means of income. You're a good if not great writer with two books to your credit, yet you have a very tough road ahead of you. What do you do? If you're smart, you go…

Indie:

So you finally nailed the big contract. Your agent just called, all out of breath and beyond excited. She can hardly wait to tell you that you have been offered $100,000 for a two book, hardback, soft, eBook, and audio world rights deal. You're about to become the darling of New York City and the talk of the town…

…Sound familiar?

You sign your contract and receive the initial $25,000 signing advance, minus the expenses to the agent and the IRS. You're left with about $16,000. For a traditional writer who has since quit his job, you're going to be depending on this cash to live on. But you're not a traditional only writer. You are a hybrid author. You publish both traditional and indie.

You enjoy multiple publishing platforms which means not only do you publish with Amazon KDP, you publish with Kobo, iBooks, and Barnes & Nobles, among others. A number of your books are enrolled in the KDP Unlimited program that offers up free books for subscribers and for which the author receives royalties on pages read. Your books are available in eBook, trade paper print-on-demand, and audio via ACX. You also have numerous books with Amazon's traditional publishing imprint Thomas & Mercer. All of these books make you monthly royalties which pay the bills and then some.

On top of this, you have five books with another traditional publisher. You have royalties coming from them every six months plus advance money still coming. You also have an agent who is constantly on the lookout for new publishing deals, foreign rights subsidiary deals, along with movie and multi-media deals. In theory, that's what the agent should be doing anyway. What all this means is, unlike the traditional publishing only writer, you haven't placed all your eggs in one basket. You are not entirely dependent on whether or not one book succeeds or fails.

If one book stinks up the joint, you have others that will take up the slack (I'm mixing metaphors, but you get it). In all reality, this is how the traditional publishing house survives. By publishing numerous titles knowing full well that 7 out of ten titles will not earn out their advance (it's probably more like 8 or 9 titles out of ten, but I'm being optimistic).

Instead of living on that $16K, you do something magical with it. You invest a portion of it into your indie books knowing you'll receive anywhere from a 20 to 30% return on investment. You invest another portion into Mutual Funds which will make you at least 5% annually. You use a little for traveling to Europe where you will live and work for a month or more, because as authors, we can take our work with us. The rest you use to pay off a bill or two, or to just piss away. It's up to you what you do with it. After all, you're a hybrid author and you and you alone are in control of your destiny.

Awards

Traditional:

Books published by traditional authors are always being nominated for awards. Everything from the Pulitzer Prize to the ITW Thriller Award (I've won the latter for my novel, Moonlight Weeps). The publishers still believe that winning prestigious awards will somehow spark a sales spike. This idea has some merit, theoretically speaking, that is. It only makes sense that a book that has won a major award would sell more units, right? The sad truth is that awards don't mean squat when it comes to sales.

Like I've already indicated, I won both the 2015 ITW Thriller Award for Best Original Paperback along with the 2014 PWA Shamus Award for Best Original PI Paperback for the same novel, Moonlight Weeps (Down & Out Books). Did I realize a noticeable spike is sales? Not at all. I have no explanation for this, other than the average reading public just doesn't care that much about awards. It might be enough to spark their interest, but I think what it all comes down to is this: readers know what they want to read and that's that. I guess, if you love medium rare steak, but the well done pork chop has won all the restaurant awards, you're still going to go with the steak.

All that said, winning big awards is a very big deal. Regardless of what they do or don't do for sales, they are a very important part of a writer's legacy. And while indie awards are becoming more and more common, it's only in traditional world that you'll be nominated for the most prominent honors. Here's what I've been nominated for and won in traditional world:

--The ITW Thriller Award for 2015

--The PWA Shamus Award for 2014

--The Amazon Editor's Choice Selection for 2013 (The Remains)

--Thomas & Mercer Kindle First Selection for Everything Burns

--Thomas & Mercer 100,000 Sales Award for The Remains

I've also had two books selected by Suspense Magazine in two separate "Best of" categories. One of these, The Shroud Key, is an indie book.

Indie:

As already indicated, more than likely you're not going to win many major awards in indie land. However, it is becoming more and more possible that you might find one of your indie books nominated for something. As more traditional authors move over to the indie side of things, this will become more commonplace. Look for an indie to win something like The Pulitzer Prize for Literature within ten years. This is not wild speculation by any means. It is instead a direct reflection of the professional publishing climate we are currently living in.

There is no mistaking the fact that traditional publishing is becoming a near impossible dream even for full-time seasoned writing veterans like myself. Unless you are a celebrity, a prominent politician, a guaranteed New York Times bestseller or the like, it is going to be very difficult if not heartbreakingly impossible to land a major deal.

It might still be possible to land a small deal with say, a $5,000 advance. But do you really want to sell all your rights for a measly 5K and a 15% royalty should you be lucky enough to earn out? In indie land, you can make a $2,000 investment to produce your book (consider that a $2,000 advance to yourself), and make all your money back within two years. From that point out, you can make a 70% royalty for the rest of your life and your grandchildren's lives. It won't be the glamorous thing to do, but financially speaking, it will be the right thing to do.

Agents

Traditional:

Some authors might argue with me, but I've been in this business now for over twenty years and I believe that in order to succeed or have a chance of succeeding in the traditional marketplace, you need an agent. Despite what you might imagine about agents as being these rich as hell, business suited men and women who strike mega deals with big New York and Hollywood on a daily basis, the actual truth is far sadder. With the dawn of indie publishing, many agents have found themselves downsizing or out of work altogether. Some agencies are merging with others in order to stay relevant. Some are even becoming micro-publishers. Why? Because authors don't need an agent in order to publish a book like they used to prior to the eBook revolution. Why give up an additional 15% if you don't have to?

But in traditional world, the top editors won't agree to read an author's novel unless it's represented by a reputable AAR (Association of Author's Representative) agent. That's the way the system has worked for more than fifty years and in terms of the big publishing houses, I don't see it changing in the near future. Your agent, if he or she is a good one, will groom your manuscript and get it "in shape" for its inevitable presentation to the big guns at the publishing houses. They will talk your project up and convince the editors that they not only can't live without your book, but that some competing house is going to snatch it up if they don't act fast.

A good agent will have a stellar reputation with the chief editors, not the low on the totem pole ones who aren't able to offer the big money. They will go to bat for your project like no other and when they sell the book, they will then hop on the subsidiary rights bandwagon and sell the foreign rights as well as the movie rights. In theory.

Word of caution: a literary agent, even a really great one, is not a magician (Although my first agent, Jimmy V, has left the publishing industry and is now a professional magician. You can't make this stuff up). He can't just wave the old magic wand and come up with a deal even if the novel is the next The Old Man and the Sea (and by the way, The Old Man and the Sea would never sell today). A publishing deal relies on many factors totally unrelated to the manuscript's worth and the author's talent. Publishers run a profit/loss statement on the book before anything else. If, in the end, the projected losses seem to outweigh the anticipated profits, your great agent is going to get an email that will go something like this: "Dear Agent, while I very much enjoyed reading your client's novel, and saw some real potential in it, I'm afraid it's not right for our publishing house. Have a nice life."

Even if it's somehow proven that your great manuscript just might produce a profit, you still have to get by the marketing department. Marketing is usually made up of young people who have their fingers on the cultural pulse. No joke. They can kill a book deal or make a book deal even if the editors don't like it. I had a two book major deal in the hand two years ago, and guess how it got shot out of the sky? The marketing department didn't like it. Not even my agent, who had a great relationship with the editor in chief, could talk the publisher into making the deal happen. Keep in mind, I've sold hundreds of thousands of books with this publisher, and they still passed. That's how competitive things have become. I published the book anyway under my own Bear Media imprint and it's doing surprisingly well and will continue to do so for years to come.

Indie:

In indie world, you do not need an agent. I repeat, YOU DO NOT NEED AN AGENT! Since you won't be shopping your books to the traditional publishers but instead, self-publishing, you can save the perpetual 15% royalty payout the agents require. That money is better served being invested in your book production which, as I mentioned before, should be earning you somewhere around 20% per year, or even better.

As a hybrid author, you can go either way. I choose to have an agent because I still seek out traditional deals. However, I am not dependent on those traditional deals. I strongly feel that mega-traditional deals, expect in a few cases, are rapidly becoming a thing of the past, making them even more like hitting the lottery. Hey, maybe hitting the lottery is easier than getting a mega book deal, these days.

But hybrid authors will also want to attempt to sell their foreign rights and movie rights. Again, in theory. Agents will often tell the indie and/or hybrid author how they will have no problem selling the foreign and media rights to your indie books, but it's absolute bullshit. Most agents never succeed at this. That said, you have to ask yourself if paying an agent 15% of your royalties is worth it.

I believe it is. However, I only pay 15% on the deals the agent makes on my behalf. I never ever pay an agent 15% of my indie eBook, audio, or paper sales. If an agent asks for that, immediately can them, and tell them I told you to do it. I'll gladly take the blame.

However, good, honest agents will go to bat for you in the rights and legal departments. If there's ever a dispute over who owns the copyright to one of your books or if, God forbid, someone sues you for liable or plagiarism, having a good, decent agent on hand is almost as good as a great lawyer, and a hell of a lot less expensive.

The Bestseller Lists

Traditional:

The major publishers might be on their way to becoming dinosaurs, but one facet of their business still holds true. They can put your book solidly on the New York Times bestseller list, if they so choose (Amazon Publishing Imprints can make your book an Amazon Kindle No. 1 Overall bestselling book, if they want). If the pubs feel invested enough in a title, and wish to make the cash investment, they can place a novel, even from a brand new author, at the number 1 spot on any of the big bestseller lists. This was how Nicholas Sparks was launched nearly twenty years ago now.

I've had the good fortune of Thomas &Mercer of Amazon Publishing launching at least two of my titles in such a way they both reached the No. 1 Overall spot on the Kindle Bestseller List. No easy feat, considering one must sell around 7,000 books in a single day in order to nail that position. If you want to stay there, you'd better be selling around 7k day in and day out. I once hit the Amazon Top Ten Overall for a two weeks straight. The only book that was in front of me at the time was John Grisham's, The Lincoln Lawyer, which at the time, was a major motion picture. This was back in 2011 when you could sell 3K copies a day and maintain that kind of superstar bestseller status. It's almost impossible for any one author to remain in the Amazon Overall Top Ten for very long now that millions of titles are being published each year.

The point is that you will have far more luck hitting all the major bestseller lists if you publish with a traditional publisher. It just depends on how much time and effort they want to put into your book.

Indie:

Forget the bestseller lists. Okay, yes you have a decent chance of hitting one or two of Amazon's niche bestseller lists, like Hard-boiled Amish mystery, or Steamy Gay Noir or, if you write non-fiction books, Gluten Free High Protein Diet Shake Books. But these lists, while exciting to land on, rarely reflect much in the way of sales. It's more a matter of the niche being so small and specialized that only a few sales will nab you a position in their top 20.

But I must admit, I recall the first time I hit one of the Amazon Bestseller lists, nearly ten years ago now. It was the first time I'd ever been associated with a bestselling anything and I was tickled pink. I remember being interviewed by the local news about the novel, Moonlight Falls (1st edition) which had been published by a very small or what's known as a micro press, and bragging about how it was an Amazon bestseller. Something I would never brag about now, unless the title were resting comfortably in the top overall Amazon Kindle100. Now that's a bestseller to be proud about because it represents real sales, not projected sales as is the case with the New York Times bestseller list.

But indie publishing, as opposed to traditional publishing, isn't about selling a lot of books in a very short time in order to grab the spotlight. It's all about the slow, steady sales. It's about taking charge of your book so that it is always selling, year in and year out. I have five titles with a medium sized house that languish in obscurity because the publisher not only doesn't promote the titles other than to feature them on social media now and again. And trust me, social media doesn't sell books. Sadly, this kind of approach is called the Toss-It-Up-Against-The-Wall-And-See-If-It-Sticks approach to publishing. Unless you are super, super lucky, it doesn't work. I've asked for the rights back to several of my titles and of course the publisher refuses. What they are doing is collecting publishing rights, sitting on them, and making a profit from the massive accumulation of small sales. It's highway robbery I tell yah. Oh well, I guess nobody put a gun to my head when I signed the contracts, so I have no one to blame but myself.

To make it in indie world, you must rise above the noise. You must invest in...

Promotions

Traditional:

Like I've already discussed ad nauseam, the traditional publishers can solidly place your novel on the New York Times bestseller list should they choose to do that. Or, they can allow your novel to slip on through the cracks, so that it immediately sinks into the abyss. This is the risk you take when you cash that advance check. Part of the problem in traditional world is this: it takes a really long time for your novel to be published. From the moment you sign your contract to publication date can be as long as a year and a half (I once heard of one author's pub date being pushed out to two years!). In that time, things change. Maybe your type of novel is no longer as popular as it was when the publisher took it on. Or maybe your acquiring editor has pulled an Elvis and left the building for good, effectively orphaning your novel (this has happened to me twice and both times the novel tanked). Maybe the marketing department is no longer into the book like they initially were. Maybe some new hotshot author has come along since you signed, and she's being hailed as the new JK Rowling. Or maybe your publishing house gets swallowed up by another larger house in a consolidation, and the original editorial and creative staff you started off with are let go prior to the book's publication (this has also happened to me).

The point is that any number of factors can kill your book's chances for success even before it gets out of the starting gate. In traditional world, unless you put up thousands of dollars for an outside publicity firm, chances are, your sales will be humble. It's important to keep in mind that any money you pour into publicity will likely result in a poor ROI. If anything, you will be lining the pockets of your publishers if something works. Example, I put up $1,150 for a BookBub promotion…arguably the Holy Grail of eBook promotions…for my novel Orchard Grove, and not only did the publisher not reimburse me for the expense, they gladly profited off the promotion. Yup, I took that one right up the bum as they say. But again, lesson learned.

Indie:

Control is the first word that comes to mind here. You, as author and publisher…you as the king or queen of your empire…you alone control just how much money you are willing to invest in both promotions and marketing packages. You can invest in any number of promotion sites, like Kindle Daily Nation, or Bargain Booksy, or of course, BookBub (if they'll have you), and make your book an Amazon Bestseller, at least in the short term.

If your book is enrolled in KDP Select, you can enjoy Kindle Countdown Deals and five free days per three month period. These are invaluable tools for building your audience. You can make the first book in a series permafree, thus enticing readers who stand the chance of being turned into fans who will go on and devour the rest of your series. You can join BookFunnel and build your subscriber list which, as time goes by will become your pot of gold. In a word, the more subscribers who belong to your tribe and your brand, the more books you will sell. You can blog, make YouTube videos (I suck at this), take on speaking gigs, run blog tours, make video trailers, run Facebook and Amazon Marketing Services advertisements…the sky is the limit to how much marketing you can do. It's all up to how much you're willing to spend and what your estimated ROI turns out to be.

I hang a calendar on my office wall and each month I plan out which promos I'm running and when. Strategic placement is key. For instance, you'll want to run a flash sale on a Friday when people are buying books for the weekend, then continue to push that flash sale all weekend long. You'll also want to run a Kindle Countdown Deal on a Friday maybe in conjunction with a Bargain Booksy. There are several wonderful books that go into depth on the subject of how to market your indie books. Just go to Amazon and enter the topic into the search engine and you'll see what I mean.

One last note on indie promotions. Just recently I started hiring outside firms to take care of both building my subscriber list and running BookBub-like ad promotions. As of this writing, the jury is still out on both, but thus far, I have been averaging 200-300 new subscribers to my newsletter per month which is not too shabby. As for the new BookBub-like promotions, we'll have to see. But the NYC-based professional running the show seems more than willing to put his money where his mouth is. Let's just hope he puts some money in my bank account.

Making a Living

Traditional:

It's a sad fact that even some of the most popular writers who publish traditionally exclusively, still need to subsidize their income with either a part-time gig like teaching for instance, or even a full-time job (see Financials). Many of the most popular authors you see sitting out on the front table at the local Barnes and Nobles, excepting the Steven Kings and James Pattersons (Patterson hires freelance writers to flesh out his books), often ghostwrite for other popular authors. This can be a lucrative but unforgiving business.

Back in the very early 2000s when I was living exclusively in traditional world, I was paid $50,000 and sent on an all-expenses paid global research trip to places like Greece, Turkey, Paris, London, to write a full-length novel about the Elgin Marbles. The man who hired me was a wealthy Texas public relations and advertising mogul who had orchestrated President George Bush Sr.'s first senatorial bid. His summer house in Kennebunkport was located directly across the street from the Bushes who were steadfast family friends.

While the project initially started out on good terms, it all went bad some six months into it when my employer kept rejecting material that might be offensive to his friends the Bushes, or the Marcus's (of Stanley Marcus stores), or the Pecks (as in Gregory Peck), and God knows who else. Being that I was dependent on partial payments of $12,500 apiece per accepted portion of novel, I had basically become this multi-millionaire's indentured servant.

I eventually quit the project having received 2/3rds of my money. Or was I fired? I can't remember which, but to this day I still have nightmares about that ghost project. It was only some years later on that I'd heard similar horror stories from some of my novelist friends.

I think it was an article published recently either in the New York Times or The Guardian that stated traditionally published authors average about $8,000 per year in income. My guess is that number isn't far off. A word of caution to all you would-be Great American novelists: Even if you receive a high mid-six figure advance for your book, you should think twice about quitting your day job. Or, if you quit you job, then by all means, go Hybrid. You're going to need the money.

Indie:

Indie world has treated me quite well over the past 9 years since I was first introduced to eBooks and the Kindle. Prior to that, I'd gone from working with the majors and being treated like a rock star to being relegated to working with a micro publisher for zero advance. It was like a major league All Star baseball player being busted to the minor leagues. By all accounts, I probably should have given up on any notion of ever being a full-time author again. Indeed, my second wife left me because my career was in the dumper. She did come back around again when I'd once more become a major success and in turn I dedicated quite a few novels to her. Sadly, it didn't last for reasons I'll explain in a bit.

My income in 2010 for my fiction was around $600 and change. In 2011, that fiction income shot up to around $30,000 and in 2012 I think I doubled that. Same for 2013 and 2014. In 2015, things began to slow a little bit while Amazon shifted their Kindle Unlimited model from being paid for the entire book to $.0045 per page read. This one little paradigm shift really put a dent in a lot of indie and hybrid author's annual income.

But for writers like me who are prolific, it's a matter of writing more books. In indie and hybrid world, content is still king. The more products you have to sell in your shop, the more money you're going to make. Build up your subscriber list while marketing smartly and you should eventually see success. Unlike the traditional world where the men and women running the publishing house want to see short term if not immediate success or you're out on your ear, the indie world is all about slow, steady growth. What's the secret to that success? Write, publish, rinse, repeat. That's the formula, no magic or luck required.

Part III

In conclusion and some (shocking) advice (bulleted)

I've experienced some real ups and downs in my 20+ years in this crazy publishing business. Here's what I've learned above all else: if there's one thing you can count on, it's constant change. I've been writing and publishing long enough to pretty much see it all. This is a volatile business that all too often defies even simple logic. For instance, how can anyone expect a title to succeed if it's not advertised aggressively and marketed smartly? You can ask that of a publisher until you're blue in the face and they'll just shrug their shoulders and smile stupidly.

Listen, if a novel is a success, the publisher almost always takes a whole lot of the credit. But if a novel tanks, it's always, and I mean *always*, the author's fault. Get used to it. And what is a successful author exactly? One who hangs in there and never gives up. An author who writes his stories no matter what's happening in the industry, no matter what's going on in his life. He writes because the writing is the one thing he can control. Authors who can't weather the storms are the ones who will eventually quit and fade into history.

Trust me, I've seen a whole lot of writers come and go through the years. Every now and then I come into contact with one, and they nearly always pat me on the back and tell me what an inspiration I am. Not really, I tell them. I write because that's all there is for me. I can't imagine doing anything else with my life.

So then, I promised you some advice. This is more for the younger, newbie crowd but there's a few gems that everyone can take away.

--Read. Read a lot. Read what you love. If you're going to write hard-boiled mysteries, read a ton of hard-boiled mysteries. Get a feel for the rhythm and the story arc. If you're not reading, you're not learning.

--Write everyday. Write everyday even if you have a day job and kids under foot. Find the time to do it. A good idea is to get your butt out of bed early in the morning, even if it hurts. That's how I wrote my first stories. By getting up at 430AM, morning in and morning out. Consider it paying your dues.

--Simplify your life. More times than not, there's not a lot of money being made in the fiction writing business. Pay off your debts and use cash whenever possible. Sell your house, and move into an apartment. Houses are a time and money suck. Cars are a money suck too. Sell the BMW and get something that you can pay for outright.

--Don't get married. Yup, you read that right. Don't get married. You will be married to your work (You'll recall my ex and her comment about the writing and traveling coming first). Date, get some action however you can, even see someone exclusively, but don't, for the life of you, get married. If you become a full-time writer, chances are you will make a habit out of getting divorced. I've got two divorces under my belt and the writing was to blame for both of them, both directly and indirectly. My longtime love just broke up with me last year. Her reason? "Your writing and your traveling come first." Which leads me too...

--Travel. Travel like crazy. Travel even if you don't have whole lot of extra money. Go to Europe and write in the cafes. Stay in guest houses if you have to. But just go there and hook up with like-minded people. Find a city in Europe that you like, and stay for a month and just write. It will be a life changing experience. Go to crazy, out of the way places…dangerous places…write about them. Sell your articles or publish blogs pieces. Maybe John Cheever was able to write great stories about the suburbs, but chances are, you won't. Go out and gather as many experiences as you can. Be a 21st century Hemingway.

--Quit your job. If you're planning on becoming a hybrid author, and if you're reading this I can only assume you are, write a series and self-publish it. With the right marketing you will slowly build up sales and a following. You're reputation as a popular author will grow too and make you more appetizing to the publishers. As of this writing, I'm able to call a publisher and ask them to buy my book without their having even read it yet. All they required was an elevator pitch. Turns out they liked the pitch and now they want me to write a novel a year for them. Now that's clout. But it took me years to get there. But you need the time to write, so as soon as it's feasible, pay off your bills, sell the house, trade in the expensive car, and give your boss notice. Then, don't look back.

--Join a writer's meetup group. This is more important for the newbies. You're going to need feedback, and there's no quicker way to becoming a better writer than getting slammed by your peers. But…

--Don't go to Writing School. At one time, you needed writing school if you wanted to teach, which was the best thing a would-be full-time novelist enslaved to the traditional, one-novel-per-year publishing system could ever hope for. But the one book a year thing no longer holds true thanks to indie publishing. Better that you learn by reading and writing your tail off, and getting the books out there. You will get better with experience and the writing will come easier as the years go by.

--Exercise. You're gonna be sitting on your ass a lot. How did Papa Hemingway put it? Writing and traveling broaden the mind, but they also broaden your ass. Something like that anyway. And for some reason, writers love to eat and drink. Especially drink. Booze seems to go hand in hand with putting words on a page. In any case, you'll need to stay healthy and in fighting shape. So get yourself into a workable daily exercise routine. Your heart, mind, and waistline will thank you for it.

--Remove all the Neg Heads from your life. This almost goes without saying. Despite enormous cultural and societal changes in the 21st century, people still fear those things they don't understand. When you make that crucial decision to give up the conventional life for the life of a writer, you will be looked upon with suspicion at best, and scorn at worst. Even your friends, who deep down inside hate going to their 9-5 jobs day in and day out, will treat you poorly. Dump them. Get rid of them, cast them aside, you don't need their negativity in your life. You are trying to build a career in an incredibly difficult and competitive field. You will need all the positive energy you can get.

--Don't write to market. Too many writers are chasing after their own tail in a desperate attempt to figure what will be the next big trend. That's a fool's errand. Maybe you think vampire dolphins is all the rage today and you hustle out a novel called, "Dolphin Blood Lust." You either publish it yourself or you nab a traditional deal. But the book tanks. How can that be? What sells today won't necessarily sell tomorrow. Do yourself a huge favor and write what you love to read. The book will read better because you will have not only poured your heart and soul into it, but you have had fun writing it, and that fun will show itself on the page.

--Be patient. This is the last bit of advice I'll offer up for now, but it is quite possibly the most important. I know it's become something of a cliché, but sometimes clichés serve an important universal purpose. Being successful as a full-time hybrid author is not a race. It is not a sprint. It is a marathon of slow but steady output and sales. Don't pay attention to your sales ranks. Don't pay attention to sales other than at the end of every month. Focus on averages, not one specific point in time. Obsessively checking your amazon rankings is like looking at a clock. It might be 1:14 right now, but that's just one isolated moment in time. It's the same with your ranks. They are fluid and constantly changing and adjusting. All you need to do is check out the monthly stats on your books. If a few are struggling, enter them into some promos and get them going again. Think like a business person, not a sensitive artist. Think long term, not one week out, or a month out, or even three month's out.

Think five years out.

I hope you've enjoyed this book about the Hybrid Author Mindset. I didn't set out to write a full book, just a short article. But this happened instead and I'm happy for it. I guess I've gained a decent amount of experience during my 20+ year long publishing journey and I've only been too happy to pass some of it on to you. Now go put out that word count and publish traditionally and independently. Never put all your eggs in one basket. Develop those multiple streams of passive writing income and you will find that you can not only live a beautiful life of freedom, you can work from anywhere in the world.

Speaking of which, I just booked my flights to Italy. I'll be heading to Florence for a month and half where I'll be writing a new book while seated inside a café, energized by way too many espressos and the joy of just being alive and lucky enough to spend my life doing what so many others only dream about.

Happy writing! Happy publishing!

If you enjoyed this book please check out some of Vincent Zandri's bestselling fiction such as Arbor Hill and The Guilty. Or for more essays on writing and the writing life, grab Vince's Pieces of Mind: Fictional Truths & Non-Fictional Lies about Writing and the Writing Life. Remember to go to WWW.VINZANDRI.COM to grab all the Zandri novels and stories and to grab your FREE copy of Moonlight Falls.

Allow me to thank you ahead of time, for your honest review of this book!

Winner of the 2015 PWA Shamus Award and the 2015 ITW Thriller Award for Best Original Paperback Novel for MOONLIGHT WEEPS, Vincent Zandri is the NEW YORK TIMES, USA TODAY, and AMAZON KINDLE No.1 bestselling author of more than 125

novels and novellas, including THE REMAINS, THE SINS OF THE SONS, THE SHROUD KEY and THE FLOWER MAN.

Said to be one of the most prolific writers of his generation, Zandri's list of domestic publishers includes Delacorte, Dell, Down & Out Books, Thomas & Mercer, Polis Books, Oceanview Publishing, Blackstone Audio, and Suspense Publishing. An MFA in Writing graduate of Vermont College, Zandri's work is translated in the Dutch, Russian, French, Italian, Japanese, and Polish.

Zandri was the subject of a major feature by the New York Times and he has also made appearances on Bloomberg TV and FOX news. In December 2014, Suspense Magazine named Zandri's, THE SHROUD KEY, as one of the "Best Books of 2014." Recently, Suspense Magazine selected WHEN SHADOWS COME as one of the "Best Books of 2016". A freelance photo-journalist he is the author of the host of The Writer's Life YouTube Channel. Zandri has written for Living Ready Magazine, RT, New York Newsday, Hudson Valley Magazine, Writers Digest, The Times Union (Albany), Game & Fish Magazine, Strategy Magazine, and many more. He lives in Albany, New York and Florence, Italy.

For more go to WWW.VINZANDRI.COM.

Vincent Zandri © copyright 2018, 2023

All rights reserved as permitted under the U.S. Copyright Act of 1976. No part of this publication may be reproduced, distributed, or transmitted in any form or by any means, or stored in a database or retrieval system, without the prior permission of the publisher. The only exception is brief quotations in printed reviews.

Bear Media 2023

http://www.vinzandri.com

Author Photo by Jessica Painter

The characters and events portrayed in this book are fictitious. Any similarity to a real person, living or dead is coincidental and not intended by the author.

Published in the United States of America

www.ingramcontent.com/pod-product-compliance
Lightning Source LLC
Chambersburg PA
CBHW030510220526
45464CB00006B/2741